Diana Krauss

111 Steps to open the Heart

Unlock the power of your heart with 111 easy steps

Impressum

Author:
Diana Krauss, Emil Teubner Strasse 27
08280 Aue

© 2023 Diana Krauss
Produced and published by:
BoD – Books on Demand, Norderstedt
ISBN: 9783757829933

MIX
Papier aus verantwortungsvollen Quellen
Paper from responsible sources
FSC® C105338

FSC
www.fsc.org

Foreword

What if there was a guidebook to help us survive and thrive in this fast-paced, often overwhelming modern world? Diana Krauss, a renowned healer, master chef, and holistic health coach, who has developed a comprehensive guide to opening your heart and living a deeply fulfilling life. With 111 steps to guide you on your journey, this book is a must-read for anyone seeking greater joy, purpose, and fulfilment in their lives.

Through a series of easy-to-follow steps, this book teaches the importance of self-love, forgiveness, and embracing vulnerability. Krauss combines her spiritual teachings with her culinary expertise, offering nourishing recipes and food rituals to enhance the journey towards heart-centred living. Packed with wisdom, guidance, and practical tools, "111 Steps to Open the Heart" is an essential read for anyone seeking greater self-awareness, peace, and joy in their lives.

It's a must-read for anyone seeking to enhance their emotional intelligence and improve their relationships. Whether you're seeking to heal your heart, deepen your spirituality, or simply cultivate more joy and meaning in your daily life.I hope that this book inspires you to embark on a journey of self-discovery and love, and I wish you all the best in your own unique path.
Love, Diana

Chapter 1

Chapter 2

Nurturing the Heart trough Selfcare

Chapter 3:

Establishing a Gratitude Practice

Chapter 4:

Showing Kindness to Others

Chapter 5:

Practicing Forgiveness and letting go

Chapter 6:

Cultivating Compassion

Chapter 7:

Connecting with Nature and the Elements

Chapter 8:

Engaging in Creative Activities and Play

Chapter 9:

Practicing Mindfulness and Presence

Chapter 10:

Building Strong Relationships

Chapter 11:

Heal your Past

Chapter 12:

Serving others and Contributing to the World

Chapter 1

Introduction

In 111 Ways to Open Your Heart," author, chef and spiritual teacher Diana Krauss provides a comprehensive guide to discovering the many paths to enhancing emotional well-being.

After two major transformative experience, something shifted within me and my heart opened wide.

This experience allowed me to see the world in a completely new way and altered my perspective on life.

I found myself feeling more loving, connected and vulnerable than ever before. Through this experience, I learned to embrace the unknown, trust the journey and live fearlessly from my heart. It brings me immense joy and fulfilment to share my knowledge and experiences with you in the hopes that you too can navigate the path of love. There is no greater pleasure than seeing others learn and grow from the lessons I've gained along the way. I hope that you will find value in what I have to offer and that it

may aid you in your own journey towards true love and happiness.

Why is it so important to open the Heart?

Opening the heart is important as it allows a person to experience love, compassion, and empathy towards themselves and others. An open heart enables one to develop deeper connections in relationships, improve communication skills, and increase emotional resilience. It also promotes acceptance, forgiveness, and the ability to let go of negative emotions.

Additionally, studies have shown that opening the heart can also have physical benefits, such as reducing stress and improving overall heart health.

A closed heart in this world means someone who is not open to others, who may be distant or disconnected from those around them. They may be guarded or hesitant to reveal their emotions or thoughts, making it difficult for others to connect with them on a deeper level. A closed heart can lead to isolation, loneliness and an inability to form meaningful relationships. It is important for individuals with closed hearts to work on unlocking their emotions and practicing vulnerability in order to form healthy connections with others.Therefore, practicing techniques such as meditation, mindfulness, and gratitude can help open the heart and lead to a more fulfilling life.

Chapter 1

Nurturing the Heart trough Selfcare

Practising self-care is important for maintaining good physical, emotional and mental health. Taking time to make healthy food choices, getting enough sleep, and engaging in regular physical activity can help improve physical well-being.

1. Start a daily meditation practice

Starting a daily meditation practice can help open your heart by increasing self-awareness, reducing stress, and cultivating a sense of compassion and empathy towards yourself and others. Studies have shown that meditation and mindfulness practices can also improve emotional regulation, boost feelings of happiness and contentment, and strengthen interpersonal relationships. Ultimately, cultivating an open heart through meditation can lead to greater levels of well-being, fulfillment, and connection with the world around you.

Start a daily meditation practice, follow these steps:

Choose a time and place:
Pick a time of day when you can commit to a daily practice and choose a quiet place where you will not be disturbed.
Sit comfortably: Find a comfortable seated position. You can sit on a cushion on the floor, in a chair with your feet flat on the ground, or even lie down.

Set a timer:
Set a timer for a comfortable amount of time (even 5-10 minutes is a great start). As you become more comfortable with meditation, you can gradually increase the time.

Focus on your breath:
Close your eyes and focus on your breath. Take deep breaths in through your nose and exhale through your mouth. Try to keep your mind focused on your breath.

Notice when your mind wanders:

It is natural for your mind to wander during meditation. When this happens, simply notice it, and gently bring your attention back to your breath.

<u>Be consistent:</u>
Consistency is key when developing a daily meditation practice. Try to meditate at the same time every day to help make it a habit.

<u>. Be patient:</u>
Meditation is a practice, so don't get discouraged if it feels difficult or your mind wanders. It takes time and patience to build a regular meditation practice, but the benefits are worth it.

2. Practice positive Affirmations.

Practice of positive affirmations opens the heart because it encourages individuals to focus on and acknowledge their positive qualities and experiences. This helps to shift their mindset towards positivity, building a strong sense of self-worth and self-esteem. Positive affirmations also promote self-love and acceptance, which in turn opens up the heart to giving and receiving love. When our hearts are open, we are more able to connect deeply with others and experience genuine compassion and empathy. Overall, the practice of positive affirmations can lead to a more positive and fulfilling life, both individually and in relationships with others.

Affirmations:

"I am worthy of love and I give love with an open heart."

"My heart is open to receiving love and blessings from the universe."

"I forgive myself and others, allowing love to flow freely through my heart."

"I release any fear or mistrust and trust in the power of love to guide me."

"My heart is filled with gratitude and joy, attracting positive energy and experiences."

3. Attend a Sound Bath.

Attending a sound bath to open the heart can be a unique and transformative experience that may help individuals connect more deeply with themselves and others.

Why people attend sound baths?

1. To release negative emotions:
The vibrations and sounds of the instruments can help release emotional blockages that may be preventing the heart from opening fully.

2. To deepen relaxation and reduce stress:
The meditative quality of sound baths can help calm the mind and reduce stress, promoting a more open and receptive state.

3. To increase self-awareness:
The experience of a sound bath can help individuals become more present in the moment, increasing self-awareness and allowing for a greater connection to the heart.

4. To enhance compassion and empathy:
When the heart is open, we may feel more compassionate and empathetic towards others, as well as towards ourselves

4. Do Yoga

For many, living with an open heart refers to forming loving relationships with friends, family, and romantic partners without fear, judgment, or grudge-bearing. However, in ancient traditions such as yoga, the heart represents far more than relationships with others; it is the doorway to the soul itself. In yoga, heavy emphasis is placed on heart opening, a practice that has a profound number of physical, emotional, psychological, and spiritual benefits. Indeed, heart opening yoga poses can act as the gateway to our deepest vulnerabilities.

5. Take a Osho Medidation Class

Osho meditation techniques can help individuals to relax and let go of their worries. When we are less stressed, we are more likely to feel open and connected to others. Osho meditations often involve self-reflection and introspection. By becoming more aware of our own thoughts, emotions, and behaviours, we can learn to accept ourselves and others more fully.

When we hold onto negative emotions like anger, resentment, or fear, our hearts can feel closed and guarded. Osho meditations like cathartic breathing and emotional release practices can help individuals release these blockages and feel more open and connected. Opening the heart can also help us build stronger connections with others. n essence, taking an Osho meditation class can be one way to embark on a journey of self-discovery and personal growth towards emotional and spiritual well-being.

6. Getting enough rest and sleep

Getting enough sleep and rest is crucial for opening the heart in multiple ways. First, it helps to reduce stress and regulate hormone levels in the body, making it easier to experience positive emotions such as joy and love. Additionally, adequate sleep and rest provide the body with the healing and rejuvenation it needs to function optimally throughout the day. This results in greater physical and emotional wellbeing, which in turn makes it easier to connect with others on a deeper level and cultivate meaningful relationships. Overall, prioritizing rest and sleep creates a foundation for a healthier and more open-hearted life.

7. Eat a lot of nutritious Food

Eating nutritious food can help open the heart by providing the essential nutrients required for optimal physical health. A well-balanced diet that includes fruits, vegetables, lean protein, and healthy fats can lower the risk of heart diseases, maintain healthy blood pressure and cholesterol levels, and reduce inflammation. Physically feeling good and healthy can translate into a positive mindset, leading to an open-hearted approach to life. Additionally, sharing healthy meals with loved ones can also deepen social connections and foster emotional well-being, further opening up the heart.

Recipes to open the Heart

1.Lentil and Spinach Soup:

This hearty soup is packed with iron and potassium, helping to regulate heart health.

Sauté 1 chopped onion and 1 garlic gloves with 300g lentils, add in 1 canned tomatoes, and vegetable broth.

Simmer until lentils are tender.

Add 2 cups fresh spinach.
Season with vinegar, curry powder, sugar, salt and chilli flakes.

2. Quinoa and Roasted Beet Salad

Quinoa is a fantastic source of fiber, magnesium, and protein, working together to keep the heart healthy.

Combine cooked 300g quinoa
with 200g roasted beets,
pumpkin seeds,
and 150g feta cheese.

Drizzle with a citrus vinaigrette,
mix 1 cup fresh strawberries with 1 Tablespoon honey
and 50 ml Balsamic Vinegar .
Add 150 ml Oliveoil
and 150ml Pomegranate Juice.
Season to taste.

8. Take silence for a day.

Taking silence for a day can open the heart because it allows us to quiet the mind and connect with our inner selves. In the absence of external distractions and noise, we become more aware of our thoughts, emotions, and feelings. We can reflect on our lives, our relationships, and our goals, and gain insight into who we are and what we really want. This can increase our empathy, compassion, and understanding of others, and help us to be more present and mindful in our daily lives.

9. Just smile

Smiling is a powerful way to open our hearts to others. The simple act of smiling communicates warmth, openness, and acceptance, which can make us feel more connected to the people around us. Smiling also releases endorphins, the body's natural feel-good hormones, which can make us feel better and more positive. In addition, when we smile at someone, we are sending a signal that we are approachable and friendly, which can make them more likely to approach us. So by smiling, we can open our hearts to others and create a more positive atmosphere.

10. Surround yourself with positive people.

Surrounding oneself with positive people can have a significant impact on one's mental and emotional well-being. Being in the presence of people who exude positivity can increase one's own optimism, reduce stress levels, and improve overall happiness. Positive people can also provide encouragement, support, and motivation, helping individuals to pursue their goals with greater confidence. Conversely, being around negative people can drain one's energy, lower self-esteem, and increase feelings of anxiety and depression. It is important to cultivate relationships with those who bring out the best in us and uplift our spirits.

11. Take a break from technology.

Taking a break from technology can open the heart because it allows individuals to disconnect from distractions and focus on themselves and others. It provides an opportunity to be more present in the moment and engage in meaningful conversations and connections without the constant interruption of screens and notifications. This can lead to increased empathy, compassion and understanding, thus opening the heart to new experiences and deeper connections with others. Additionally, taking a break from technology can reduce stress levels and improve overall well-being, leading to a greater sense of happiness and fulfillment.

12. Set intentions for your day

Setting intentions for your day opens the heart because it allows you to tap into your innermost desires and values. When you set an intention for your day, you are consciously choosing to focus your mind and energy on something meaningful and important to you. This brings clarity and purpose to your day, which can uplift and inspire you. Additionally, setting intentions encourages you to be present and mindful, which can help you connect with your emotions and bring greater awareness to your heart. Ultimately, setting intentions for your day is a powerful way to cultivate a more loving and compassionate heart.

Setting intentions for the day can help to bring focus and purpose to your daily activities.

Here are three ways to set intentions for the day:

1. Practice gratitude and set an intention for the day: Begin your day with appreciation for the blessings in your life, and then set an intention for the day based on what you want to achieve or how you want to show up in the world.

2. Meditate and visualize your day: Spend some time meditating to clear your mind, and then visualize how you want your day to unfold. Imagine yourself succeeding in your tasks, and connect with the feelings of accomplishment and satisfaction.

3. Write down your goals and priorities: Take some time to write down the most important tasks and goals that you want to achieve for the day. Then, prioritize them according to their importance and impact. This will help you stay focused and on track throughout the day.

Chapter 3:

Establishing a gratitude practice

To establish a gratitude practice, start by setting aside a specific time each day to reflect on things you are thankful for. This could be done through journaling, meditating, or simply speaking aloud. Focus on both big and small moments of gratitude, such as a loved one's support or a beautiful sunset.

13. Cultivate a gratitude Journal.

Cultivating a gratitude journal involves regularly writing down things we appreciate and feel gratitude for in our lives. This simple practice can have a profound impact on the heart, as it encourages us to focus on the positive aspects of life and appreciate what we have. By consciously recognising and acknowledging the good things in our lives, we increase feelings of positivity and promote well-being. This positive shift in perspective also opens the heart to greater empathy and compassion towards ourselves and others, fostering deeper connections and relationships.

To cultivate a gratitude journal, there are three steps you can follow.

1.

Set aside some time each day to reflect on things you are thankful for. This could be anything from a helpful colleague to a beautiful sunset.

2.

Write your thoughts down in a notebook or app. This will help make your gratitude more tangible and consistent.

3.

Regularly review your journal to remind yourself of the positive things in your life. Practicing gratitude this way can help you feel happier and more content.

14. Write a love letter to yourself.

Writing a love letter to yourself is a valuable exercise in opening your heart. It allows you to practice self-love and compassion by acknowledging your unique qualities, strengths, and accomplishments. By expressing gratitude and positive affirmations, you can boost your self-confidence, self-esteem, and emotional well-being. Additionally, it can help release negative self-talk and limiting beliefs, paving the way for growth, healing, and self-acceptance. Ultimately,

writing a love letter to yourself is a powerful tool to cultivate a deeper connection with your true self and enhance your overall happiness and fulfillment in life.

15.Practice saying "thank you" more often

Practicing saying "thank you" more often is important to open the heart because gratitude is a positive emotion that can enhance our well-being and deepen our relationships with others. When we express gratitude, we acknowledge the good things that others do for us, which can increase our sense of empathy, compassion, and connection with them. Additionally, gratitude can help us focus on what we have, rather than what we lack, which can promote a more positive and optimistic outlook on life. By making a habit of saying thank you more often, we can cultivate a grateful mindset that opens our hearts to the abundance and beauty of the world around us.

7 Ways to say thank you

Thank you for your help.
I really appreciate it, thank you.
Thank you so much for your time.
Thank you for being there for me.
I'm grateful for your support, thank you.
Thank you for your kindness.
I'm so thankful for everything you do.

16. Express gratitude for what you have right now.

Gratitude is the key to happiness, and it's important to appreciate what you have right now. Start by reflecting on all the blessings in your life, big or small. Write them down and thank the people who have made them possible. Take time to cherish the moments that bring you joy, and recognize the lessons learned from hardships. Cultivate a daily gratitude practice, such as naming three things you're thankful for each morning or keeping a gratitude journal. Remember, life is a gift, and expressing gratitude for what you have right now can bring you inner peace and contentment.

17. Be great full and bless your Food

Being grateful and blessing your food is a way of acknowledging and showing appreciation for the resources that have gone into the meal. It is also a way of expressing gratitude towards the people who have contributed to the production, transport and preparation of the food.

Blessing your food can also help to create a moment of mindfulness and reflection before you eat, allowing you to fully appreciate and savor the nourishment and flavors of your meal.

Expressing gratitude before meals is a common practice in many cultures and can help to cultivate feelings of contentment and connection with others.

Beeing grateful is also a way to show appreciation for the nourishment that it provides to your body. By taking a moment to acknowledge this, you become more mindful of what you are eating and can develop a healthier relationship with food.

Exercise:
1. Offer a simple prayer or blessing before eating, expressing gratitude for the food and those who prepared it.

2. Take a moment to let the aroma and appearance of the food inspire appreciation and thankfulness.

3. Consider making a donation or volunteering at a local food bank or charity as a way of giving back and showing gratitude for the abundance in your life.

18. Reflect on the good things that happened during the day

It helps us cultivate a sense of gratitude for the positive experiences we have had during the day. Gratitude has been shown to have numerous benefits for our mental and physical health.

Reflecting on the good things helps us to focus on the positive aspects of our day rather than dwelling on the negative. This helps us to develop a more positive mindset and attitude towards life. Remembering the good things that happened during the day can boost our self-esteem and confidence. It reminds us of our positive qualities and accomplishments. It help us to reduce stress and feel more relaxed. This can have a positive impact on our overall well-being. Overall, reflecting on the good things that happened during the day is an important practice that can help us to cultivate happiness, positivity, and gratitude in our lives.

19. Practice self-reflection.

Self-reflection is a powerful tool that can help individuals enhance and gain a better understanding of their own thoughts, attitudes, and behaviors. Through self-reflection, one can identify their strengths and weaknesses, understand their emotions and decision-making process, and develop a clearer sense of their purpose and values. Regular self-reflection can improve self-awareness, boost personal growth, and aid in decision-making, problem-solving, and goal-setting. By making self-reflection a habitual practice, individuals can foster a sense of inner peace and stay aligned with their goals and priorities.

1. Journaling:
Writing down thoughts, feelings, and experiences can help identify patterns of behavior and emotions.

2. Mindfulness:
Being present in the moment and noticing thoughts and feelings without judgment can provide insight into patterns of behavior and help promote self-awareness.

3. Seeking feedback:

Asking for constructive feedback from trusted sources can help identify blind spots and offer a different perspective on behaviors and actions.

20. Challenge yourself to be great full in difficult situation

It is important to challenge yourself to be grateful in difficult situations because it helps in developing a positive attitude and outlook towards life. Being grateful means focusing on the things you have, rather than the things you lack. It can help you shift your perspective and find solutions instead of giving up or feeling overwhelmed. Gratitude also promotes resilience and improves mental health by reducing stress and anxiety. By challenging yourself to be grateful in difficult situations, you can train your mind to see the good in every situation and appreciate the small things in life.

Gratefulness Practise

1. Start by setting aside time every day to reflect on the things you are grateful for.

2. Write down at least three things that you are thankful for, even if they are small things like hearing your favorite song on the radio or having a good cup of coffee in the morning.

3. When facing a difficult situation, challenge yourself to find something positive in the situation and add it to your journal. For example, if you're stuck in traffic, you might be grateful for having time to listen to a new podcast or audiobook.

4. Read through your gratitude journal regularly to remind yourself of all the things you have to be grateful for.

5.This exercise trains your mind to focus on the positive aspects of any situation and helps shift your perspective from a negative one to a more optimistic one.

21. Practise gratitude for others

Showing gratitude to the people around you can help you open your heart to those who you may have taken for granted. Whether it's thanking a coworker for their help or expressing your appreciation to a loved one for their support, acknowledging the positive impact someone has had on your life can deepen your connections and bring joy to those around you. So take a moment today to express your thanks and gratitude to those who have touched your life, and let your heart overflow with appreciation and love.

Step 1:
Take time to reflect on the people in your life

Step 2:
Write down specific things you appreciate about them and what they have done for you

Step 3:
Reach out to that person and express your gratitude either in person, via phone call, text or email. Let them know how much they mean to you and how thankful you are for them. This will not only make the other person feel good, but also strengthen your relationships.

22. Gratitude Medidation

Gratitude meditation is a type of mindfulness meditation that focuses on cultivating gratitude and appreciating the positive aspects of one's life. Here are the steps to practice a gratitude meditation:

1. Find a comfortable and quiet place to sit or lie down.

2. Take several deep breaths and allow your body to relax.

3. Bring to mind something that you are grateful for. It could be a person in your life, a specific experience, or even something as simple as a beautiful sunset.

4. As you focus on this grateful feeling, allow your body to soak it in. Feel the warmth and expansion in your heart, or wherever the feeling arises in the body.

5. Begin to mentally list other things in your life that you are grateful for. You can use categories like friendships, work, home, health, or hobbies to guide you.

6. For each thing you list, pause and allow yourself to feel the gratitude. Imagine the positive impact it has had on your life.

7. Continue this practice for as long as feels beneficial, but aim for at least 5-10 minutes.
8. When you are ready to finish, take a few more deep breaths and allow your body to relax once again.

Chapter 4:

Showing Kindness to Others

Showing kindness to others can take many forms. It can be as simple as giving someone a compliment or holding the door open for them. Even small acts of kindness can make a big difference in someone's day.

23. Smile at strangers and say hello.

Smiling at strangers and saying hello is a way to build connections and promote positivity in the world. When we smile at someone and say hello, we acknowledge their presence and show that we are approachable and friendly. This creates a sense of community and can improve our mood and outlook on life. Showing kindness to others also promotes a sense of empathy and connection, even with people we may not know. Over time, these small acts of kindness can lead to greater feelings of happiness, fulfilment, and belonging. By opening our hearts to others, we may also feel more connected to the world around us, and ultimately, feel more fulfilled and satisfied with our lives.

24. Offer to help someone who is struggling with a task.

Offering to help someone who is struggling with a task can show kindness, compassion, and empathy. It can also create a sense of community and support, which can promote feelings of trust and belonging. Additionally, helping someone in need can be a rewarding experience, both for the person offering the help and the person receiving it. Assisting others can also encourage a positive attitude and build stronger relationships. Overall, offering to help someone who is struggling with a task can be impactful and could make a difference in someone's life.

25. Give compliments and acknowledge the positive qualities of others.

By recognising and appreciating the positive qualities of others, you are more likely to establish and maintain positive relationships with them. This creates a sense of trust and respect between you and the other person. Compliments and positive acknowledgments help to boost the self-esteem of others. When someone receives positive feedback, it reinforces their confidence in themselves and their abilities. When someone is acknowledged for their positive qualities, it encourages them to continue to develop those qualities. Doing so can help them to grow and improve themselves. When positive feedback is given in communication, it can create a more open and understanding environment. This can lead to improved communication and more productive interactions. Overall, acknowledging the positive qualities of others is an important part of building and maintaining healthy relationships and promoting personal growth and development.

26. Listen and show empathy towards someone who is going through a tough time.

By actively listening and empathising, you are showing the person that their feelings and experiences are valid, and that they are not alone in what they are going through. Sometimes, all someone needs is someone to listen and understand without judgment. It can help someone feel supported and cared for. When someone feels heard and understood, it can alleviate stress and anxiety, and reduce the risk of depression. By listening actively and showing empathy, you are building a deeper relationship of trust between you and the person going through a tough time. When someone feels heard and supported, they may be more likely to open up and communicate about their struggles, which can lead to finding solutions and getting help.

27. Write a thoughtful note or card to someone who has impacted your life in a positive way.

Writing a thoughtful note or card to someone who has impacted your life in a positive way is important for several reasons: A handwritten note or card is a meaningful way to express your gratitude for the positive impact someone has had on your life. It lets the person know that you appreciate and cherish them and their contributions to your life. Taking the time to write a thoughtful note or card shows that you value the relationship with the person and want to maintain and strengthen it. It can also make the person feel valued and cared for, which can deepen the connection between you two. Sending a positive message can brighten someone's day and spread positivity and happiness. By sharing your positive thoughts and feelings, you can inspire the person to continue making a positive impact on others.

A thoughtful note or card can serve as a meaningful keepsake that the person can treasure for years to come. It can also inspire them to continue doing good in the world, knowing that their efforts have made a positive impact on someone's life.

Overall, writing a thoughtful note or card to someone who has impacted your life in a positive way is an excellent way to express gratitude, strengthen relationships, boost positivity, and leave a lasting impact.

28. Simply treat everyone with respect and kindness, regardless of their background or circumstances.

Treating everyone equally without any biases or prejudices creates a sense of fairness and equality among people. It helps in breaking stereotypes and discrimination based on race, gender, religion, or other factors. Respectful and kind behaviour fosters positive relationships with people, helps in building trust and mutual understanding, and leads to a more peaceful and inclusive community. By displaying respectful and kind behaviour, you set an example for others to follow. Your actions may inspire others to do the same, creating a positive ripple effect that can contribute to a better society. Treating others with respect and kindness can also help to improve your own character. By practicing these values, you can become a better person and improve your relationships with others.

Overall, treating everyone with respect and kindness is essential for creating a more harmonious and inclusive society where everyone feels valued and appreciated.

29. Do something unexpected and kind

I decided to surprise my neighbor who has been feeling a bit down lately. I went to the local bakery and bought her favorite pastry, a warm croissant, and a bouquet of fresh flowers. I knocked on her door and when she opened it, I simply told her that I wanted to brighten her day and handed her the goodies. She was so surprised and grateful, and it felt amazing to spread a little bit of kindness in my community.

1.Pay for the person's meal behind you in a drive-thru or at a restaurant.

2. Leave a handwritten note of encouragement or gratitude on a coworker's desk or a stranger's car.

3. Offer to run errands or do tasks for an elderly or disabled neighbour who may struggle with these tasks on their own.

Chapter 5:

Practicing Forgiveness

Practicing forgiveness allows us to release ourselves from hurt and pain caused by others. It involves acknowledging our emotions and choosing to move forward without resentment or anger towards the offending party. Practicing forgiveness is a powerful way to cultivate inner peace and improve relationships. Here are the exercises you can try:

30. Acknowledge the emotional pain to understand

When we recognise and accept our emotional pain, we can begin to process and work through it. Ignoring or denying our emotions may lead to psychological distress and negative outcomes. Validating our emotions also helps us connect with others who may be going through similar situations and feel less alone. By understanding our emotional pain, we can learn from it and make positive changes in our lives.

31. Connect with your higher self

Forgiveness is a key element in personal growth, healing, and spiritual development. When we forgive, we release ourselves from negative emotions like anger, resentment, and bitterness, and we create space for positive emotions such as love, compassion, and inner peace. Forgiveness can be challenging, but by connecting with our higher self, we tap into our higher wisdom, intuition, and spiritual guidance, which can help us see things from a broader perspective and approach forgiveness with openness, compassion, and understanding. Our higher self is the part of us that is connected to the divine, and accessing it through meditation, prayer, or any other spiritual practice can help us cultivate forgiveness as a spiritual virtue and a way of life. In this sense, connecting with our higher self to practice forgiveness is not only important for our own growth but also for the well-being of others and the world around us.

32.Acceptance the emotional pain

Acceptance of emotional pain is important in the process of forgiveness because it allows an individual to fully acknowledge and experience the hurt that was caused. By accepting the pain, they can then begin to let it go and move forward, rather than suppressing or denying it which can lead to unresolved feelings and potential resentment. The acceptance of emotional pain also allows individuals to gain perspective on the situation and understand that forgiveness is a choice they are making for their own wellbeing, rather than condoning or excusing the behaviour of the person who caused the harm.

33. Write a forgiveness letter.

Writing a forgiveness letter to yourself can spark a transformational healing process and open the heart Writing a forgiveness letter to yourself can spark a transformational healing process and open the heart to self-love and acceptance. By acknowledging our flaws and mistakes and offering ourselves genuine apologies and compassion, we can release the burdens of shame and guilt that keep us stuck in the past. This process allows us to cultivate a new relationship with ourselves built on forgiveness, kindness, and understanding.

Ultimately, it can help us move forward with more confidence, resilience, and inner peace.

Dear Self,

I know I have caused you pain and let you down in the past. It is time to let go of those mistakes and forgive myself. I am sorry for the pain I have caused and promise to do better in the future. I will no longer hold onto resentment towards myself and instead fill my heart with love and compassion. I am worthy of forgiveness and I choose to let go of the past and embrace a brighter, more loving future.

With love and forgiveness,
(Your Name)

34.   Let go of resentment and negative Emotions

Holding onto resentment and negative emotions can keep us stuck in a negative state of mind. It can also create a barrier around our hearts, preventing us from fully experiencing positive emotions and connecting with others. Letting go of these negative feelings allows us to release ourselves from their grip and open our hearts to new possibilities. It can also lead to improved relationships and a sense of inner peace and happiness. Ultimately, releasing resentment and negative emotions is a crucial step towards living a more fulfilling and joyful life.

Focus on positive affirmations, gratitude, and self-care, such as meditation or exercise, to promote inner peace and calmness. Practice empathy and understanding towards others and prioritise building healthy relationships. Remember that holding onto negative emotions only harms yourself and the people around you, so choose to let go and embrace positivity.

35. Learn what Forgiveness means to you

To learn what forgiveness means to you, take time to reflect on what it means to let go of resentments and anger towards someone who has wronged you. Consider the emotional and mental weight lifted when you forgive someone. Think about how it improves your relationships and overall well-being. Forgiveness can mean different things to different people, so it's important to define it for yourself. Look to your values and beliefs to guide you in determining what forgiveness looks like for you personally. Practice forgiving yourself and others to deepen your understanding and experience of forgiveness.

36. Practice forgiveness towards yourself

Forgiveness is the key to opening your heart. Practicing forgiveness towards yourself and others allows you to let go of negative emotions and cultivate compassion. Holding onto grudges and resentment only serves to create barriers and blockages in your relationships. Forgiving yourself for past mistakes and forgiving others for their transgressions can be challenging, but it is necessary for healing and growth. By shifting your perspective towards forgiveness, you can release the weight of the past and embrace a more open and loving heart.

Practise forgivness

1. *Reflect on your own experiences with forgiveness. Think of times when you forgave someone else or when someone forgave you. What was involved in the process for you? How did it feel afterward? What did you learn from the experience?*

2. *Read and research about forgiveness. Look for books, articles, or podcasts that discuss forgiveness and what it means. Take notes on what you learn and reflect on how it relates to your own experiences.*

3. *Talk to others about their experiences with forgiveness. Ask friends, family members, or a*

therapist to share their stories with you. Listen carefully and ask questions to understand what the process meant to them.

4. Practice forgiveness. Look for opportunities in your life to practice forgiveness, whether it's forgiving someone who hurt you or working to forgive yourself for a mistake. Reflect **on how the experience feels and what it means to you.**

5. **Write about forgiveness. Take time to write in a journal** about what forgiveness means to you. Consider your own experiences and what you've learned from others. Write about what forgiveness looks like in your life and how it impacts your relationships and overall well-being.

37.   Repeat a forgiveness Mantra

Repeat this mantra to yourself:

"I forgive myself and others for any past hurts and mistakes. I release the hold that anger and resentment have on me. I choose to embrace compassion and understanding. I am free to move forward with love in my heart." Repeat as often as needed to help release any negative emotions and promote forgiveness. Remember, forgiveness is a journey and it takes time. Be patient and kind with yourself, and continue to repeat the mantra until you feel a sense of peace.

38.   Hoponopono medidation

Ho'oponopono meditation is a powerful technique used to release negative emotions, heal relationships and manifest positive outcomes. It involves repeating four key phrases: I'm sorry, please forgive me, thank you, and I love you. By reciting these phrases, the individual takes responsibility for their part in any negative situation and seeks forgiveness from the universe, allowing for healing and transformation. The practice is rooted in Hawaiian culture, promoting forgiveness and reconciliation as pathways to inner peace and harmony with others. This meditation is simple yet profound, and can be used to bring about profound healing in various aspects of life.

Chapter 6:

Cultivating Compassion

Cultivating compassion involves actively seeking to understand and alleviate the suffering of others, even when it is outside of our own experience. It requires a willingness to put ourselves in someone else's shoes and offer them kindness and support.

39. Random acts of Kindness

Practising random acts of kindness increases compassion and opens the heart to others. It helps to break down barriers and reminds us of our shared humanity. These acts can be as simple as holding the door open for someone or paying someone a compliment. Research has shown that acts of kindness also have positive benefits for our own mental and physical health, reducing stress and increasing happiness. By making kindness a habit, we can create a positive ripple effect in our communities and make the world a better place.

This can involve small gestures such as giving someone a compliment, holding the door open for someone, or buying a coffee for a stranger. These acts can help cultivate empathy and gratitude while also brightening someone's day.

40. Cultivate compassion every day

Cultivating compassion on a daily basis brings numerous benefits to both ourselves and others. It can improve our emotional well-being, reduce stress, and increase a sense of connection and empathy towards those around us. Compassion also helps create a positive environment and enhances relationships with others. It can inspire acts of kindness, deepen our understanding of diverse perspectives, and encourage us to give back to our communities. By making compassion a daily habit, we can create a more compassionate world and contribute to making a positive impact in the lives of others.

To cultivate compassion every day, start by setting an intention each morning to be kind and compassionate to yourself and others. Practice mindfulness, being present with each person you interact with and truly listening to their needs. Reflect on opportunities to help others, whether it be through a kind word, a generous act, or simply offering a listening ear. Exercise empathy by putting yourself in other's shoes and imagining what it would be like to experience their struggles.

41. Listen generously

Listening generously is an essential way of showing compassion towards others. When we listen attentively to someone without interrupting or judging, we demonstrate that we care about their thoughts, feelings, and experiences. It creates a safe space for people to open up and share their struggles, and it allows us to understand their perspective better. By practicing active listening and showing empathy, we can offer emotional support to those who need it the most. Generous listening demonstrates our desire to connect with others on a deeper level, and it is a powerful tool for creating meaningful relationships.

42. Practice empathy

To practice empathy, start by actively listening to others and trying to understand their perspective without judgment. Put yourself in their shoes and ask open-ended questions to gain a deeper understanding of their feelings and experiences. Show that you care by offering support and validation, and avoid dismissing their emotions or offering unsolicited advice. Practice kindness and compassion in your interactions, and strive to be more aware of your own biases and prejudices that may hinder your ability to empathize with others.

43. Heal your trauma

Healing from past traumas can help us become more compassionate and empathetic towards others. When we have unresolved trauma, it can create a barrier that prevents us from truly connecting with others and understanding their experiences. However, when we work through our traumas and develop a sense of self-awareness, we can begin to see others with greater understanding and openness. This can help us respond to others with greater kindness, empathy, and care, which can not only benefit our relationships but also contribute to making the world a more compassionate and loving place.

44. Loving-kindness meditation

Loving-kindness meditation aims to cultivate a sense of compassion towards oneself and others. The practice typically begins by focusing on oneself and repeating phrases such as "may I be happy, may I feel safe, may I be healthy and strong." Then, the focus is gradually extended to people close to us, acquaintances, and even those we may have conflicts with. The intention is to develop feelings of love, kindness, and empathy towards all beings. Research suggests that this meditation can increase positive emotions, improve relationships, and reduce symptoms of depression and anxiety.

Medidation:

Find a comfortable seated position, close your eyes, and take a deep breath.
Begin by envisioning yourself in a warm embrace, feeling loved and cared for.
Repeat the phrase, "May I be happy. May I be healthy. May I be loved. May I be at peace.
" Visualise these words like a golden light filling your body, surrounding you with positivity.

Next, extend this loving-kindness to someone you love, repeating the same phrases.
Finally, extend it further to someone you have difficulty with or someone you do not know.
Repeat this practice every day to cultivate a more loving and compassionate mindset.

45. Self Compassion medidation

Begin by finding a comfortable position, sitting or lying down.
Close your eyes and take a few deep breaths. As you inhale, imagine breathing in compassion and kindness. As you exhale, imagine letting go of any stress or negativity.
Bring to mind a situation where you felt self-critical. Acknowledge the pain and discomfort that arises. Repeat to yourself, "May I be kind to myself in this moment."
Visualise a warm and loving feeling spreading throughout your body. Allow yourself to feel compassion for yourself.
When you are ready, gently open your eyes and take a few more deep breaths before continuing with your day.

46. Self-compassion practice

Self-compassion practice involves treating oneself with kindness, understanding, and acceptance. It starts with acknowledging our pain or struggles and comforting ourselves as we would a close friend. This practice includes being mindful and non-judgmental regarding our emotions, thoughts, and circumstances, recognising that suffering is a normal part of the human experience. It also involves validating our own feelings, being patient and forgiving with ourselves, and practicing self-care. By developing self-compassion, we can cultivate greater resilience and emotional well-being, improve our relationships, and experience greater overall happiness and life satisfaction.

47. 21 day compassion challenge

The 21-day compassion challenge involves committing to small acts of kindness and empathy towards oneself and others for three weeks. The challenge aims to cultivate a daily practice of compassion, which can help reduce stress and increase happiness and connection with others. Each day, you are encouraged to perform a different act of compassion, such as sending a kind message to a friend or practicing self-care. The challenge can be done individually or with a group, and resources and support are available to help participants stay on track and inspired throughout the process.

21 day Compassion Challenge

1. Practice active listening with someone who needs to be heard.

2. Write a heartfelt message to someone who has positively impacted your life.

3. Express gratitude to a service worker or caregiver who often goes unnoticed.

4. Perform a small act of kindness for someone in your community.

5. Practice self-compassion by taking time to do something you enjoy without guilt or judgment.

6. Practice forgiveness by letting go of a grudge or offering an apology.

7. Engage in a conversation with someone who holds a different viewpoint than you and try to understand their perspective.

8. Donate to a charity that aligns with causes you care deeply about.

9. Offer a sincere compliment to someone who may be in need of a confidence boost.

10. Practice empathy by putting yourself in someone else's shoes and trying to understand their perspective.

11. Support a friend or loved one going through a difficult time by simply being present and offering emotional support.

12. Practice mindfulness and be present in the moment, allowing yourself to fully experience emotions and sensations without judgment.

13. Volunteer your time to a local organisation or non-profit working towards positive change.

14. Read or listen to stories about people who have overcome adversity and use their stories as inspiration for your own journey.

15. Practice generosity by giving away something you no longer need or use to someone who could benefit from it.

16. Write a thank you note to someone who has supported you in a challenging time.

17. Offer to help a neighbour or friend with a task or project they may be struggling with.

18. Practice non-judgment and avoid making assumptions about someone's situation or behaviour.

19. Engage in a dialogue with someone who has a different cultural background than you and learn about their experiences and traditions.

20. Practice patience and understanding in a situation where you may normally feel frustrated or annoyed.

21. Repeat a self-compassionate mantra or affirmation to yourself throughout the day to cultivate feelings of self-kindness and love.

Chapter 7:

Connecting with Nature and the Elements

Connecting with nature can have numerous benefits, including reducing stress, improving mental health, boosting creativity, and increasing physical activity. Connecting with nature is an important way to improve overall wellbeing. Here are some exercises to connect with nature:

48. Smell on Flowers

The smell on flowers is a natural fragrance that is directly associated with the natural world. The aroma of flowers connects people to nature, which helps to open the heart and make individuals feel more relaxed and at ease. The scent of flowers often causes people to become more mindful, which leads to an appreciation of the beauty and wonder of the natural world. Overall, the captivating aroma of flowers plays an essential role in creating a serene and peaceful environment, which can have a significant impact on mental and emotional well-being.

49. Go for a swim in a Lake or River

Taking a dip in a natural body of water like a lake or a river can be a fantastic way to connect with nature. The experience of swimming amidst the serene surroundings of a river or lake can be extremely calming and refreshing, helping to release mental stress and improve overall well-being. Additionally, swimming in natural water bodies offers a fantastic opportunity to observe and interact with local flora and fauna, adding a unique and enriching element to the experience. Whether you're looking for a solo meditative swim or a fun activity with friends, a dip in a lake or river can be a great way to unwind and reconnect with nature.

50. Hike in the mountains or forests

Hiking in the mountains or forests can be a powerful way to connect with nature. The fresh air, stunning views, and peaceful surroundings can provide a much-needed break from the hustle and bustle of daily life. It's a chance to slow down, breathe deeply, and appreciate the natural beauty all around us. Whether you're in search of a challenging workout or a relaxing stroll, there are trails for every level of hiker. So grab your hiking boots and get ready to explore the great outdoors in a whole new way.

51. Watch wildlife in their natural habitat

Observing wildlife in their natural habitat is a great way to connect with nature. It allows us to witness the beauty, diversity, and behaviour of animals and plants in their ecosystem. Watching the interaction between different species and their environment can be fascinating and educational. It also brings a sense of peace and calmness, reminding us of the natural world's balance and harmony. Whether it's spotting a majestic eagle soaring in the sky or seeing a family of deer grazing in the woods, watching wildlife in their natural habitat is an unforgettable experience that can install a deep appreciation for the world around us.

52. Sleep Outside

Sleeping outside is an excellent way to connect with nature and its spirits. It allows you to immerse yourself in the beauty of the natural environment and feel its energy. By embracing the calming sounds and stillness of the forest, you become one with the natural world. The experience can be grounding and grounding, and it offers a welcome break from the hustle and bustle of city living. Camping or sleeping outdoors is an opportunity to disconnect from technology and experience a simpler way of life, rejuvenating both the body and mind.

53. Stargazing at Night

Stargazing at night is an activity that brings people closer to nature. It allows them to observe the vastness and beauty of the skies, which can be a humbling and awe-inspiring experience. The act of observing the stars connects us to the natural world and reminds us of our place in the universe. Additionally, stargazing often takes place in quieter, remote locations away from the hustle and bustle of everyday life, which provides a peaceful environment and encourages reflection and contemplation. All of these factors combine to create a profound and meaningful connection to nature.

54. Cook a wild plants Meal

Cooking a meal with wild plants can be an exhilarating experience that connects you with nature and open the heart. As you search for and harvest the plants, you become more attuned to your surroundings and the environment. Then, as you prepare and cook the meal, you gain a newfound appreciation for the different textures and flavours of these natural ingredients. Eating the finished dish is a reminder of the interconnectedness of all living things and the importance of respecting and preserving the natural world. Trying new recipes with wild plants can be a fun and educational way to deepen your connection to nature and yourself.

Wild Plant Quiche Recipe:

Preheat the oven to 350°F.

In a bowl, whisk together 4 eggs, 1 cup of milk, and 1/2 teaspoon of salt.
Sauté 1 cup of wild ramps and 1 cup of chopped dandelion greens until tender.
Pour the egg mixture into a pie crust and add the sautéed wild plants.
Top with 1 cup of shredded cheese.

Bake in the preheated oven for 30-35 minutes or until the quiche is set and the crust is golden brown.
Let it cool for 5 minutes, slice, and serve.

Dandelion Pesto:

- 2 cups packed dandelion leaves
- 1/2 cup walnuts
- 1/2 cup grated parmesan cheese
- 1/2 cup olive oil
- 2 garlic cloves
-         Salt and pepper to taste

Blitz all ingredients in a food processor until smooth. Serve with pasta or as a dip.

Wild Nettle Soup

- 4 cups of young nettle leaves
- 1 chopped onion
- 2 chopped garlic cloves
- 2 cups of vegetable broth
- 2 cups of water
- 2 tbsp of olive oil
- Salt and pepper to taste

1. Wash and chop the nettle leaves.
2. Heat the oil in a pot over medium heat and add the onions and garlic. Cook until soft.
3. Add the nettle leaves and cook for 5 minutes.
4. Add the broth and water and simmer for 15 minutes.
5. Blend the soup until smooth and season with salt and pepper.

55. Hug a tree

Hugging a tree can provide a simple and effective way to connect with nature and promote a feeling of calm and relaxation. Trees have a calming effect on our bodies and minds, as they release organic compounds into the air that can help improve our mood and reduce stress levels. Hugging a tree can also help us to feel more grounded and connected to the earth, and remind us of the beauty and importance of the natural world around us. So go ahead and embrace a tree today – your body and mind will thank you for it!

56. Medidation to connect with the spirits of nature

Begin by finding a quiet and peaceful outdoor location where you can sit comfortably. Close your eyes and take several deep breaths, focusing on the sensation of the air entering and leaving your body. Picture the natural world around you, and visualise yourself surrounded by the lush greenery, the cool breeze, and the soothing sounds of nature. Allow yourself to connect with the spirits of the natural world, feeling their presence and their energy. Breathe in positivity and exhale negativity, letting go of any stress or tension. Continue to sit in silence, basking in the beauty of nature, and the connection you have created.

Chapter 8:

Engaging in Creative Activities and Play

Engaging in creative activities can have numerous benefits, such as providing a sense of accomplishment, reducing stress and anxiety, improving mood and boosting cognitive function.

57. Concious Drawing, Painting

Drawing and painting can help to open the heart by providing an outlet for self-expression. When we create art, we tap into our emotions, allowing us to express ourselves in ways that words cannot always capture. This can be a cathartic experience, allowing us to process difficult emotions and connect with our inner selves. Additionally, creating art can also be a meditative practice, helping to quiet the mind and promote relaxation. Ultimately, drawing and painting can help us connect with our deepest emotions and find a sense of inner peace and fulfilment.

58. Crafting

Crafting can be a therapeutic and meditative practice that allows individuals to connect with their creative side. Engaging in crafting can help to soothe anxiety, reduce stress, and promote feelings of relaxation and calmness. Moreover, crafting can require a lot of focus and attention, redirecting the mind away from negative thoughts. This can open up the heart, allowing for more positive emotions to flow in. Overall, crafting can be an excellent way to balance the mind and spirit, and to promote greater emotional wellbeing.

59.Learn Cooking

Cooking is considered a therapeutic and soulful activity that helps one express their creativity and emotions through food. Preparing a meal with love and care not only nourishes the body but also the heart and soul. Sharing a meal that one has cooked with others can foster strong, meaningful connections and create a sense of community and warmth. Cooking for one's loved ones is also a way of showing affection and care. Ultimately, cooking lets us tap into our emotions, creativity, and compassion, allowing us to open our hearts to others and ourselves.

Start by finding some basic recipes and ingredients to practice with. Follow the recipe carefully, and pay attention to cooking times and temperatures. As you become more comfortable, experiment with adjusting seasonings or adding your own twists to the recipe. Watch cooking shows, read cookbooks, and take cooking classes to learn new techniques and gain inspiration. Don't be afraid to make mistakes – cooking is all about trial and error. With time and practice, you'll soon become a confident and skilled home cook.

60. Try Acting

Acting requires vulnerability, empathy and emotional expression, which can help individuals tap into their emotions and connect with their inner selves. By diving into various roles, actors can gain a deeper understanding of the complexities of human emotion and behaviour. This emotional exploration can help individuals to release pent-up feelings, overcome emotional blocks and achieve a greater sense of personal growth. Therefore, trying acting can help open the heart by allowing people to explore their emotions, empathise with others and connect with their authentic selves.

61. Make Pottery

Making pottery is a meditative and therapeutic practice that can help open the heart. As you get lost in the creative process, you become more present and focused, allowing yourself to let go of stress and worries. The act of holding clay with your hands also connects you to your inner self and your emotions. It gives you a safe space to explore and express them. In turn, this experience can help you feel more compassionate, empathetic, and open towards yourself and others, leading to a more open heart.

62. Read books that inspire you.

Reading books that inspire you can have a transformative effect on your life. These books have a way of opening your heart, allowing you to see yourself and the world in a new light. They touch on universal themes and experiences, tapping into our shared humanity and igniting empathy and compassion. These stories offer hope, provoking us to believe in ourselves and dream big. They teach us how to overcome adversity, build resilience, and stay true to our core values. Reading books that inspire us is a powerful way to connect with our emotions, cultivating a greater sense of purpose and meaning in life.

63. Attend a spiritual Retreat.

Attending a spiritual retreat can be a great way to open your heart to new experiences and ways of thinking. By disconnecting from the stresses of daily life and immersing yourself in a peaceful, reflective environment, you'll have the opportunity to explore your spirituality and connect with your inner self. Retreats often provide guided meditations, yoga classes, and other activities that can help you feel more cantered and focused. Whether you're looking to deepen your existing spiritual practice or start exploring a new path, a retreat can be a powerful tool for personal growth and self-discovery. Being surrounded by positive energy and attitudes can uplift and inspire individuals, leading to a more open and receptive heart. Positive people can provide support, encouragement and motivation, which can boost self-esteem and confidence. Additionally, being in the presence of positive people can reduce stress and anxiety, and promote feelings of happiness and well-being.

64. Take up Gardening.

Taking up gardening can open the heart in multiple ways. Firstly, it allows individuals to connect with nature, providing a peaceful and calming environment that reduces stress and anxiety levels. Secondly, gardening is a physical activity that not only promotes fitness but also releases endorphins, the "feel-good" hormone that elevates mood and reduces pain. Lastly, gardening is a creative activity that promotes mindfulness and boosts self-esteem, providing a sense of accomplishment and purpose. By nurturing and interacting with plants, individuals can experience a deeper connection with themselves, the environment, and the world around them, leading to a more open heart.

65. Jewellery making

Jewellery making is a creative and meditative activity that can help to open the heart by allowing individuals to express their emotions and tap into their inner selves. It requires focus and concentration, which can ease stress and anxiety, allowing individuals to be more in touch with their emotions. Moreover, creating something by hand provides a sense of accomplishment and can boost self-esteem, which also helps to open the heart.

Furthermore, the act of giving jewellery as a gift can deepen connections and relationships, enhancing feelings of love and generosity.

66. Dance to uplifting music.

Dancing to uplifting music can have a positive impact on our emotional wellbeing. It has been shown to release endorphins, which are natural mood-boosting chemicals in the brain. This can open up the heart to feelings of happiness, gratitude, and love. When we dance to music that resonates with us, it can also help us connect with our emotions and process feelings that we might be holding onto. By lifting our mood and opening our hearts, uplifting music can bring a sense of inner peace and contentment.

Exercise

1. Move with the beat: Uplifting music often has a clear and consistent beat, which means you can move your body to it. Start by swaying your hips from side to side and gradually add in arm movements and footwork.

2. Use your body to express the lyrics: Uplifting music often has positive and inspiring lyrics, so use your body to express the meaning of the words. You can

*use big arm movements to show strength or jump
and spin to express joy.*

*3. Get creative: Don't be afraid to get creative with
your dance moves. Experiment with different styles
and incorporate your own unique flair. Dancing to
uplifting music should be a fun and liberating
experience, so let loose and enjoy yourself!*

67. Learn to play a musical instrument.

Learning to play a musical instrument has been shown to open the heart in several ways. Firstly, it allows individuals to express themselves creatively, which can lead to a greater sense of personal fulfillment and emotional release. Additionally, playing music requires listening and responding to others, which encourages empathy and social connection. The act of playing music has also been shown to lower stress levels and promote relaxation, leading to a more open and receptive state of mind. Overall, learning to play a musical instrument can help individuals develop a greater sense of emotional intelligence and connection to the world around them.

Chapter 9:

Practicing Mindfulness and Presence

Mindfulness is the art of being present in the moment and fully aware of one's feelings and surroundings. To practice mindfulness, one can start by focusing on breathing and staying aware of the present moment. It is helpful to choose a quiet place for practicing and avoid distractions.

68. Mind Mapping

Mind mapping exercises can be a powerful tool to cultivate presence and open the heart. By creating a visual map of thoughts, ideas, and emotions related to the heart, we can explore our feelings and connect with our inner selves. This process can help release blockages, increase self-awareness, and foster compassion for ourselves and others. With practice, mind mapping can become a regular practice to promote emotional healing and spiritual growth.

Mind mapping is a brainstorming exercise that helps to visualise ideas and connections between them. It involves creating a web-like structure of keywords and interconnected phrases to outline a concept or plan. This exercise is useful in opening up the heart and releasing creative energy, as it allows people to freely express and organize their thoughts. By mapping out ideas in a non-linear way, one can gain a deeper understanding of their ideas, increase productivity, and tap into their creativity. Mind mapping exercises are an effective tool for problem-solving, planning, and generating new ideas.

Mind mapping exercise

1.   *Mind mapping exercise: Start by writing "Open Heart" in the centre of a blank page. Then, branch out and jot down all the feelings and emotions associated with an open heart. Examples could include love, compassion, forgiveness, vulnerability, and empathy. Next, connect these*

*concepts together, exploring how they relate to each
other and how they might be interwoven.*

*2.   Draw a tree-like structure and label each
branch with a different person or group of people in
your life. Write down all the memories, qualities and
characteristics that you appreciate about each of
these people. This exercise will help you reconnect
with your feelings of gratitude and love towards
others.*

69. Fantasy Journey

Fantasy Journey is a powerful exercise that can help to open the heart. This practice encourages individuals to connect with their emotions, thoughts, and inner wisdom, which can lead to greater self-awareness and compassion. By exploring our inner landscape and acknowledging our vulnerabilities, we can begin to release any blockages that prevent us from experiencing deep love and connection. Overall, practicing Fantasy Journey can lead to greater emotional intelligence, resilience, and joy.

Fantasy journey

*One Fantasy Journey exercise for opening the heart
could be to visualize yourself standing in a beautiful
garden or meadow.*

Picture the sun shining down on you, and feel its warmth spread throughout your body.
As you take deep breaths, imagine your heart opening like a flower, radiating light and love.

Another exercise could be to visualise a loved one or close friend, and envision sending them positive energy and love from your heart.
Lastly, consider visualising yourself surrounded by a circle of supportive and loving individuals, and feel their love wash over you, filling your heart with warmth and gratitude.

70. Do Yin Yoga

Yin Yoga is known to be effective in opening the heart chakra, which is responsible for our ability to give and receive love, compassion, and kindness. The slow and steady movements in Yin Yoga help release the tension and tightness in the muscles surrounding the chest, shoulders, and upper back, which can often lead to feelings of emotional blockages. By holding stretches for several minutes, the body and mind can connect to a deeper level, allowing for deeper emotional release and a sense of openness in the heart.

Ying Yoga Poses

Reclining Bound Angle Pose (Supta Baddha Konasana):

Lay on your back with the soles of your feet touching and knees apart. Place one or two blocks or pillows under your spine at heart level to allow the chest to open up.

Sphinx Pose (Salamba Bhujangasana):

Lie on your stomach with your forearms on the mat under your shoulders, elbows pulled in. Gently press into your forearms to lift your chest off the ground.

Child's Pose (Balasana):

Bring your knees wide and big toes together, sinking your hips back onto your heels. Extend your arms forward and rest your forehead on the mat. Focus on deep breathing into the back of your heart.

71. Breath Awareness

Breath awareness is a simple and effective exercise to help open the heart. By focusing on your breath and bringing your attention to the present moment, you can cultivate a sense of calm and relaxation. This can help release any tensions or blockages in the heart center and allow for greater emotional openness and connection with others. Practicing breath awareness regularly can help promote overall well-being and a deeper appreciation for the present moment.

Breathwork

1.Sit in a comfortable and quiet space, close your eyes, and focus on your breath. As you inhale, visualise filling your heart with love and compassion. As you exhale, imagine releasing any tension or negativity from your heart space.

2. Practice pranayama (yogic breathing) exercises such as alternate nostril breathing or Ujjayi breath, which can help calm the mind and open the heart.

3. Incorporate mindful movement, such as yoga or tai chi, into your daily routine to bring awareness to your breath and body. As you move through each posture, focus on your breath and sense the opening and expansion of your heart center.

72.Body Scan

Practicing exercises that focus on scanning your body can help open your heart. This exercise involves paying attention to your body, starting with your feet and working your way up to your head. As you pay attention to each body part, you may notice any tension or discomfort and consciously release it. This can help release emotional blockages and bring more awareness to your heart space, allowing for greater openness and connection with others. Regular practice of this exercise can lead to a more open and compassionate heart.

Body scan medidation

It begins with deep breathing and slowly moving your attention from your feet to your head, feeling any sensations or tension and releasing it with each exhale.

This exercise helps to increase awareness of your body, reduce stress and anxiety, and improve overall wellbeing. In addition, it can also help to open the heart and increase feelings of compassion and empathy towards others.

73. Progressive Muskel Relation

Progressive Muscle Relaxation is a great exercise that can aid in opening the heart. This exercise involves tensing and relaxing different muscle groups in the body, which helps release physical tension and emotional stress. As the tension is released, the body and mind become more relaxed and open. This exercise can be done at any time, but it is especially effective when done before bed or during a quiet, peaceful moment. With regular practice, this technique can help to improve overall well-being and create a greater sense of openness and connection in the heart.

Exercise:

1.   *Sit or stand comfortably with your back straight.*

2.   *Place your hands on your chest and take a deep breath in.*

3.   *As you exhale, imagine that all the stress, tension, and negative emotions in your chest are being released.*

4.   *With each subsequent breath, imagine your chest opening up more and more, creating space for love, compassion, and warmth to flow in and out.*

5.   *Repeat this exercise for a few minutes, focusing on the physical sensations and emotions that arise.*

74.   Cook a healthy Dish

Cooking can be an excellent way to practice awareness and presence. When we cook, we need to focus on the task at hand, paying attention to the ingredients, timing, and measurements. This requires us to be present in the moment and brings us into a state of mindfulness. By cooking our own meals, we become more connected to our food and the process of preparing it, leading to a deeper sense of appreciation and gratitude.

One simple and healthy recipe for beginners is

Roasted Vegetables.

Preheat your oven to 400°F,

*Chop your favorite veggies
(such as carrots, bell peppers, zucchini, and onion)
Into even-sized pieces,*

Drizzle with olive oil

Season with salt, pepper, and any other herbs or spices you like.

Roast in the oven for 20-25 minutes until the veggies are tender and lightly golden.

Serve as a side dish or with some cooked quinoa or lean protein for a complete meal.

This dish is easy to make, packed with nutrients, and delicious!

75. Mindfull Eating

Practicing mindfulness during meal times can lead to a more fulfilling and aware eating experience. Mindful eating involves paying attention to the smells, tastes, and textures of food, as well as being aware of hunger cues and eating at a slower pace. This practice can help one become more attuned to their body's needs and prevent overeating. Additionally, incorporating regular exercise into one's routine can also help open the heart and promote feelings of well-being. Both meditation and exercise can be powerful tools in cultivating a sense of mindfulness and overall health.

Exercise:

The mindful eating exercise is a simple yet powerful tool that can help you cultivate a deeper sense of awareness and connection with your body, food, and emotions.

Start by sitting down at a table and taking a few deep breaths to help you focus.
Before you start eating, take a moment to appreciate the food in front of you with all your senses.
Notice the colours, smells, and textures, and take a small bite, savouring each flavour.

Chew slowly and swallow, feeling the food nourishing your body.
As you continue to eat, pay attention to your hunger and fullness cues, and stop when you feel satisfied.

This practice can also help you develop a more compassionate and healthy relationship with food, reduce stress and anxiety, and improve your overall well-being.

76. Walking Medidation

Walking meditation exercise is a great way to open the heart and promote inner peace. This form of meditation involves walking slowly and deliberately while being mindful of each step and breath. It can be practiced indoors or outdoors, alone or in a group. By focusing on the present moment and being fully aware of sensations in the body, practitioners can reduce stress and anxiety, improve concentration, and develop a greater sense of compassion and empathy. Walking meditation is an effective tool to enhance overall well-being and connect with one's inner self.

Exercise:

As you walk and focus on your steps, imagine your heart expanding and filling with love, and allow that feeling to radiate outwards towards those around you. Repeat a mantra or affirmation such as "my heart is open and full of love" to reinforce this intention. This exercise can bring a sense of peace, connectedness and emotional wellbeing.

77. Smile more often

One of the simplest and most effective ways to open your heart is to smile more often. Smiling not only lifts your mood but also has a positive effect on those around you, creating a ripple effect of happiness. Additionally, regular exercise can also aid in opening the heart by reducing stress and releasing endorphins that promote feelings of well-being. Whether it's a brisk walk or a yoga class, incorporating regular physical activity into your routine can help you feel more grounded and connected to your heart center.

78. Take a break from social media

Sometimes we need to disconnect from the virtual world to connect with ourselves. Taking a break from social media can be a good exercise for our minds and bodies. In particular, it can help to open our hearts. By putting aside the distractions and comparisons of social media, we can focus on our own thoughts and feelings. This can lead to more self-awareness and self-love. Additionally, engaging in physical exercise, such as yoga or running, can also help to open our hearts and release any negative energy. Overall, taking a break from social media and prioritizing self-care can have a positive impact on our mental and emotional wellbeing.

One effective practice for taking a break from social media is to engage in regular exercise. Exercise has numerous benefits for both the mind and the body, including reducing stress, improving mood, and increasing energy levels. Whether it's going for a run, taking a yoga class, or lifting weights, incorporating physical activity into your daily routine can provide a much-needed break from screens and social media

while also boosting overall wellness. Not only does exercise give you a break from scrolling and swiping, but it also helps you connect with your body and provides an opportunity to clear your mind.

79. Helpfull Prayers

Prayer can be a powerful tool in opening the heart, whether it be through personal reflection or connecting with a higher power. It allows for a moment of stillness and connection to something greater than oneself, promoting feelings of peace and clarity. Additionally, regular practice of prayer can also help to strengthen one's sense of empathy and compassion towards others, further enhancing the heart's openness. Incorporating prayer into one's daily routine can be a beneficial exercise for both the mind and soul.

Prayers for being mindful and opening the heart could be:

"Dear Universe, please help me to be fully present in this moment, to quiet my mind and open my heart. May I feel a deep connection to all beings and embrace with love and compassion all that arises."

"Divine Source, I ask for your guidance in opening my heart and being more mindful. May I release any fear or resistance, and allow myself to receive and give love with ease and grace. Help me to live in a state of awareness and compassion."

80. Be present in the Moment

Being present in the moment helps open our heart because it allows us to let go of the past and the future. When we focus on the present, we become aware of our thoughts, emotions, and surroundings. This awareness helps us connect with ourselves, with others, and with the world around us. As we let go of our fears and anxieties, we become more open and receptive to the beauty and wonder of life. This openness allows us to experience love, joy, compassion, and gratitude, which in turn, nourishes our heart and soul.

Exercise:

1. Focus on your breath while taking deep and slow breaths.

2. Use all your senses to be aware of your surroundings and appreciate what surrounds you.

3. Practice mindfulness meditation where you actively observe your thoughts, emotions, and sensation in a non-judgmental way, helping you direct your attention to the present, improving your well-being by relieving stress and anxiety.

Chapter 10:

Building Strong Relationships

Strong relationships are essential for personal and professional growth. To build strong relationships, it is important to prioritize communication and active listening. This involves expressing oneself honestly while also taking the time to understand the perspectives and feelings of others.

81.Active Listening

Active listening is essential for maintaining healthy relationships as it enables individuals to truly empathise with and understand one another. By actively engaging in the conversation, clarifying, summarising and responding to the other person's communication, an environment of trust, respect, and transparency can e built. This encourages open communication and makes the other person feel heard and valued. Active listening also helps prevent misunderstandings and conflict by giving individuals the opportunity to clarify and correct any misinterpretations. Ultimately, active listening enhances connection, fosters closeness, and strengthens relationships.

82. Regular Communication

Regular communication is important in relationships because it fosters understanding, trust and intimacy between partners. It allows individuals to express their needs, wants and feelings, and provides an opportunity for conflict resolution. Effective communication promotes active listening, which encourages empathy and support, and helps couples to grow together. By taking the time to connect on a regular basis, couples can strengthen their bond and work together to overcome challenges, creating a happy and fulfilling relationship.

Exercise:

1.   *The "Reflective Listening" exercise involves one person expressing a concern or issue while the other partner listens and reflects the feelings and thoughts expressed. The partner can then*

respond by acknowledging their partner's feelings and offering support and solutions.

2. The "Weekly Check-In" exercise involves setting aside time each week to discuss any concerns or issues that each partner may have and to express gratitude for positive aspects of the relationship. This allows for open communication and helps prevent any issues from building up and causing resentment.

83. Spend Quality time together

Spending quality time together is important in relationships because it promotes active listening and empathy between individuals. It allows for open communication and fosters a deeper understanding and appreciation for one another. Spending time together also helps to build trust and intimacy, as well as creating shared memories and experiences. This strengthens the overall bond and connection between partners, leading to a healthier and happier relationship. Ultimately, investing time and effort into a relationship can lead to a more fulfilling and satisfying partnership.

Two exercises for spending quality time together in relationships are:

The gratitude exercise:

Take turns expressing gratitude for each other and your relationship. This can be done during a meal or any other time that you have together. By expressing gratitude, you both can focus on the positive aspects of your relationship and strengthen your bond.

The active listening exercise:

Set aside a specific time to have a conversation where one person talks and the other person listens without interruption. Then, switch roles. This exercise will help both of you practice active listening and improve your communication skills. By understanding each other's perspectives, you can improve your relationship.

84. Show Appreciation

Showing appreciation is important in relationships because it reinforces positive behaviour and strengthens the bond between partners. When individuals feel appreciated, they are more likely to continue doing things that make their partner happy. This, in turn, helps to maintain a positive atmosphere, reduces conflicts and builds trust. Appreciation can be shown through simple actions such as saying thank you, complimenting the other person, or doing something special for them. Consistently showing appreciation can have a profound impact on the longevity and quality of a relationship.

It can be as simple as saying "thank you," acknowledging someone's efforts, expressing gratitude via a heartfelt note or gift. When individuals feel appreciated, they are more likely to feel valued, understood, and loved. This strengthens the bond between partners or friends and can help create stronger foundations for future communication. Therefore, regularly expressing appreciation for one another is a vital aspect of any healthy and fulfilling relationship.

85. Work on Conflict resolution

To work on conflict resolution in relationships, it is important to communicate openly and honestly with your partner. Identify the underlying issues causing the conflict and discuss ways to address them. Listen to each other's perspectives and be willing to compromise. Use "I" statements instead of blaming your partner, and avoid using accusatory language. Finally, ensure that you both agree on solutions and follow through with them. This will help build trust and lead to a healthier and happier relationship.

Exercise:

One effective exercise *for improving conflict resolution in relationships is "active listening".*

This involves each partner taking turns sharing their perspective on the issue at hand, while the other listens actively and reflects back what they have heard.

This helps to ensure that both partners feel understood and can more easily work towards finding a solution that works for both of them.

Other exercises *include practicing empathy, identifying and communicating one's own needs and boundaries, and working together to brainstorm creative solutions to the problem.*

86. Welcome Everything

Welcoming everything in relationships is important because it allows for honest and open communication. When we accept and acknowledge all aspects of our relationships, including the uncomfortable and challenging elements, we are able to cultivate deeper understanding, empathy, and trust. This creates a foundation for stronger connections and more fulfilling relationships. By welcoming everything, we demonstrate our commitment to growth and resilience, and we are better equipped to navigate the ups and downs that come with any relationship.

87. Gratitude for each other

Practicing gratitude towards each other in a relationship fosters positive emotions and strengthens the bond between partners. It helps individuals focus on the good things about their partner and appreciate them. Gratitude also encourages open communication and enhances empathy, leading to better conflict resolution and problem-solving. Research shows that couples who express gratitude towards each other are more satisfied and committed to their relationship, and experience less stress and negative emotions. Therefore, cultivating a habit of expressing gratitude towards each other is essential for building a healthy and fulfilling relationship.

Two exercises that can help demonstrate appreciation and strengthen relationships are:

1) Expressing gratitude daily - Take time each day to express appreciation to your partner or loved ones for something they did or a positive quality they possess. This can be done through verbal communication, handwritten notes, or small gestures of kindness. Consistently acknowledging and valuing the people in your life can help create a positive and supportive environment.

2) Engaging in shared activities - Spend time doing activities together that you both enjoy. This can be anything from cooking a meal to playing a sport or taking a dance class. Participating in shared activities can lead to a greater sense of connection and can help build a stronger bond between partners or loved ones.

88. Communicate openly and honestly

Open and honest communication is vital for any relationship to thrive. By expressing one's thoughts and feelings truthfully, partners can establish trust, mutual respect, and understanding. Honest communication allows for disagreements to be resolved, misunderstandings to be clarified, and for partners to better understand each other on a deeper level. It also promotes intimacy, leading to a stronger bond between individuals. Without open and honest communication, relationships can suffer from lack of trust, misunderstandings and resentment which can lead to a breakdown in the relationship.

89. Be Authentic

Authenticity is extremely important in relationships, as it is the foundation for trust and intimacy. Being genuine and true to oneself allows for open communication and mutual respect. When individuals can be their true selves without fear of judgment, they are more likely to form deeper connections and meaningful relationships. Authenticity also allows for healthy boundaries and enables individuals to recognize when they are not being treated with the respect they deserve. Ultimately, authenticity allows for the growth and strengthening of relationships as it cultivates honesty and vulnerability.

Exercise:

One effective exercise to practice authenticity is to regularly take time to reflect on your values and beliefs. Review situations where you may have compromised or acted inauthentically, and ask yourself why and how you could have stayed true to yourself. Challenge yourself to express your true thoughts and feelings in difficult conversations. Be mindful of your actions and decisions, and check-in with yourself regularly to ensure they align with your authentic self. Remember that authenticity is a continuous journey and practice, not a destination.

90. Setting Boundaries

Setting boundaries is an important aspect of healthy relationships, both personal and professional. It involves communicating clear guidelines and limits for how you are willing to be treated or interacted with. Boundaries can be physical, emotional, or relational, and they help establish trust and respect between individuals. It's important to identify and articulate your boundaries clearly and to honor those of others. When boundaries are crossed, it's important to communicate and enforce consequences to maintain healthy relationships and mutual respect. Establishing boundaries can be uncomfortable but it leads to better communication, healthier relationships, and increased self-awareness.

Exercise:

1. *Identify your values and priorities:*
2. *Understanding what matters most to you can help you determine what boundaries you need to set to protect those things.*

2. Communicate clearly:
Be direct and explicit about your boundaries with others. Don't assume they'll know what you need if you don't tell them.

3. Practice saying "no":
Learning to say no when you need to is an important part of setting boundaries. Don't feel guilty or apologise for protecting your time and energy.

4. Take ownership of your emotions:
Setting healthy boundaries means taking responsibility for your own emotions and reactions. Don't let others dictate how you feel.

5. Practice self-care:
Prioritizing self-care is crucial when setting and enforcing boundaries. Make time for activities that nourish your body and mind, and don't sacrifice your own well-being for others.

Chapter 11:

Heal your Past

Trauma is defined as an emotional response to an overwhelming and physically or emotionally threatening event. Trauma causes the can result from adverse life events in childhood or adulthood, abuse, relationship violence, assault, loss, and more.

91. Let go of Pain

Letting go of pain is necessary for healing because it allows us to move forward without being held back by past hurts.
Holding onto pain only prolongs our suffering and prevents us from fully experiencing joy in the present moment.

By releasing the pain, we free ourselves from negative emotions and can focus on positive growth and healing. It may be difficult to let go, but it is essential for our mental and emotional well-being.

Through forgiveness, self-care, and seeking support, we can find the strength to release the pain and heal.

Exercise:

1.Mindful breathing: Focus on your breath and visualize the pain leaving your body as you exhale.

2. Progressive muscle relaxation: Tense and then relax each muscle group, starting from your toes and working up to your head. This helps release physical tension and can also calm the mind.

3. Journaling: Write about your pain, explore its roots and try to reframe your perspective. This can help you gain insight and find ways to cope and move forward.

92. Let go of Bitterness

Bitterness is like a poison that only affects the one holding onto it. Let go of bitterness and choose forgiveness. Holding onto bitterness only causes pain and resentment towards others. It's important to let go of the past and move forward with a positive attitude. This allows room for growth and healing. Forgiveness does not mean forgetting what happened, but choosing to let go of the negative emotions attached to it. Choosing to forgive allows for a happier and more peaceful life. Letting go of bitterness is essential for personal growth and well-being.

Exercise 1: Forgiveness Letter

Write a forgiveness letter to the person who caused the bitterness. Be honest about your hurt, but also express your willingness to forgive and move on. If possible, deliver the letter to the person or even just read it aloud to yourself. This exercise helps to release negative emotions and allows you to take ownership of your feelings.

Exercise 2: Gratitude Practice

Start a daily gratitude practice. Each morning or evening, write down three things you are grateful for. This exercise helps you to focus on the positive things in your life, rather than dwelling on the negative. Over time, you'll begin to see more things to be grateful for, and the bitterness will begin to fade.

93. Let go of comparing yourself with others

Comparing yourself to others can be harmful to your self-esteem and mental health. Everyone has their own unique journey and struggles, and comparing yourself to others can lead to feelings of inadequacy and negative self-talk. Instead, focus on your own accomplishments and progress, and set goals based on your own interests and abilities. Remember that success and happiness look different for everyone, and there is no one "right" path in life. Celebrate your own journey and the unique qualities that make you who you are.

94. Let go of Expectations

The burden of expectations can weigh heavy on our shoulders, causing stress and anxiety. By letting go of expectations, we can free ourselves from this burden and live more freely. It's important to remember that things don't always go as planned, and that's okay. Instead of dwelling on what should have happened, focus on what you can do in the present moment. Embrace life with an open mind, and allow yourself to be pleasantly surprised by what happens. Letting go of expectations can lead to a more peaceful and fulfilling life. Take stock of what you are expecting from yourself and others and try to understand where those expectations come from. Reframe your perspective to appreciate what is in front of you without judgement. As you let go of expectations, you may feel a newfound sense of freedom and peace.

95. Let go of Resistance

Release any resistance that is holding you back from achieving your goals. Accept that change is a natural part of life and embrace it with open arms. Trust in the process and have faith that everything is working out for your highest good. Practice mindfulness and focus on the present moment, rather than worrying about the future or dwelling on the past. Remember that you have the power to choose your thoughts and reactions, and choose positivity and gratitude over negativity and fear. Let go of any limiting beliefs and trust in your abilities to create the life you desire.

Exercise

1.   *Write down all the reasons why you're resisting something, then challenge each reason to see if it's true. Often, we resist things out of fear or false beliefs that we've constructed. By going through*

each reason with a critical eye, we can start to break down the resistance.

2. Practice mindfulness meditation to increase your awareness of the resistance you're feeling. As you meditate, pay attention to any thoughts or emotions that arise as you think about the thing you're resisting. By observing without judgment, we can start to let go of our attachments to these feelings and ultimately release the resistance.

96. Let go of Emotions

Detaching oneself from emotions can be a challenging yet rewarding process. It involves acknowledging and accepting emotions without allowing them to control one's actions or thoughts. By practicing mindfulness and developing a healthy perspective towards emotions, individuals can learn to let go of negative feelings such as anger, jealousy, and resentment, and focus on the present moment. This can lead to an increased sense of calmness and better decision-making abilities. Although it may take time and effort to master, letting go of emotions can enhance overall mental and emotional well-being.

Letting go of emotions is essential for mental and emotional well-being. Here are some ways to do so:

Exercise:

1. Acknowledge your feelings and accept them without judgment.

2. Express your emotions in a healthy way, such as writing or talking to a trusted friend.

3. Practice mindfulness and focus on the present moment rather than dwelling on the past or worrying about the future.

4. Engage in physical activity to release pent-up energy and emotions.

5. Seek professional help if necessary, such as therapy or counseling.

Remember, letting go of emotions takes time and effort, but it can lead to a more peaceful and fulfilling life.

97. Surrender

Surrendering means giving up control and accepting what cannot be changed. It is a difficult but important act that requires vulnerability and trust. Sometimes, surrendering can lead to new opportunities and unexpected outcomes. It is not a sign of weakness, but rather a strong and courageous decision to let go. Surrendering can bring peace and clarity, allowing one to move forward with renewed perspective and energy. While it may be scary, surrendering can be a transformative experience that brings growth and personal development.

Exercise:

1. Trusting the universe: Take a moment to reflect on a situation that is causing you stress or anxiety. Instead of trying to control the outcome, trust that the universe has a plan and surrender your need for control. Allow yourself to be open to whatever unfolds.

2. Letting go of expectations: Identify an area of your life where you have set high expectations for yourself or others. Practice letting go of these expectations and surrender your attachment to the outcome. Accept what is and trust that everything will work out in its own time and in its own way.

98. Visit a Healer

Sometimes it may seem like the past is too heavy a burden to bear alone. That's where healers come in. These trained professionals offer a space for individuals to explore their emotional wounds and work towards healing and growth. Healing the past is a process that can be challenging and uncomfortable, but with the help of a skilled healer, it's possible to overcome even the most difficult experiences and move forward with greater resilience and peace. If you're struggling with unresolved trauma or emotional pain, consider seeking out a healer who can guide you towards a brighter future.

To find a healer to address and heal past traumas, start by researching local therapists, counselors, and healers who specialize in trauma recovery. Look for professionals who have experience working with similar situations or backgrounds to your own. Check their reviews, credentials, and read their bios to determine if they are a good fit for your needs. You can also ask for referrals from friends or family who have sought healing for similar issues. It's important to find someone you feel comfortable with and whom you can trust to help you on your healing journey.

99. Visit a sacred space

Visiting a sacred space can be a meaningful and moving experience. Whether it be a temple, church, mosque, or other place of worship, entering a space dedicated to spirituality and higher power can create a sense of peace and connection. Through observing rituals, being surrounded by symbols and art, and engaging in prayer or meditation, visitors can deepen their understanding and appreciation of different cultures and belief systems. Moreover, such spaces often offer a respite from the chaos and stress of daily life, allowing for reflection and introspection.

The world is filled with sacred places where one can seek healing and peace. Among them are the healing springs of Lourdes in France, the ancient Salt Cathedral in Colombia, the holy town of Varanasi in India, the serene Machu Picchu in Peru, the serene Bali in Indonesia, and the spiritual Sedona in Arizona, USA. Others include Mount Kailash in Tibet, the ruins of Petra in Jordan, and the serene Uluru in Australia. These places are imbued with natural beauty, cultural significance, and spiritual power that can provide solace and renewal to those seeking healing.

100. Heart Purification Medidation

Heart purification meditation is a technique used to cleanse and clear negative emotions and thoughts from the mind and heart. It involves focusing on the heart center and visualizing a white light entering the heart, cleansing all negative energy and emotions. This technique helps individuals to let go of any resentment, anger, or fear, and promotes inner peace and emotional balance. By practicing heart purification meditation regularly, one can develop compassion, love, and understanding towards oneself and others, leading to a more harmonious and fulfilling life.

Heart Purification Meditation is a powerful technique to release negative emotions and promote positive energy.

Medidation:

Begin by closing your eyes, sitting in a comfortable position, and taking deep breaths. Focus your attention on the heart chakra, the center of love and compassion. Visualise a bright light filling your heart and surrounding your body. As you exhale, imagine releasing any negativity or stress you might be carrying. Repeat positive affirmations to yourself, such as "I am loved," "I am worthy," and "I am at peace." Continue for several minutes, allowing yourself to fully let go and experience emotional healing.

101. Heartpower Healing

Heartpower Healing offers energy healing services to help individuals unlock their inner potential for healing and self-discovery. Utilizing a combination of modalities such as Reiki and chakra balancing, they aim to release emotional and physical blockages and promote clarity, balance, and relaxation. Sessions are tailored to each individual's unique needs and can be done in-person or remotely. Founder and practitioner, Diana Krauss, creates a safe and nurturing space for clients to connect with their heart center and tap into their own innate healing abilities.

Chapter 12:

Serving others and Contributing to the world

Embracing vulnerability is an essential element in building authentic relationships and achieving personal growth. Vulnerability allows us to connect with others on a deep emotional level and fosters empathy and compassion. By being vulnerable, we show our true selves, flaws and all, which is necessary to build trust and intimacy. Moreover, it requires courage to put ourselves out there and take risks, allowing us to break out of our comfort zones and learn from our experiences.

102. Donate time or resources to a charitable cause.

One way to make a positive impact on the world is by donating time or resources to a charitable cause. Whether it's volunteering at a local food bank or donating money to a nonprofit organisation, every little bit helps.

Giving your time and skills can be just as valuable as a monetary donation, and can make a real difference in the lives of those in need. Remember, even the smallest contribution can have a big impact, so consider getting involved and giving back to your community today.

If you want to donate your time or resources to a charitable cause, here are a few steps you can take.

First, research organisations in your community or online that align with your values and interests.

Next, reach out to the organisation to inquire about volunteer opportunities or donation needs. Consider donating money, goods, or services that the organisation needs, or look for opportunities to volunteer your time and skills.

Finally, follow through on your commitment and keep in touch with the organisation to continue making a positive impact.

103. Share your knowledge or skills with someone who could benefit from it.

One of the most fulfilling things you can do is to share your knowledge or skills with someone who could benefit from it. Perhaps you have a talent for cooking, and your neighbor is struggling with putting meals together. Or maybe you're an expert in financial planning, and your friend is having difficulty managing their finances. Whatever it is, take the time to offer assistance and guidance. Not only will it benefit the person you're helping, but it will also give you a sense of purpose and fulfillment. Helping others is one of the most rewarding things you can do in life.

104. Feed the Hungry

Feed the Hungry is a noble cause that has a significant impact on the world. Hunger is one of the most pressing issues that affects millions of people across the globe. By supporting organizations that help provide food to the needy, we can make a positive difference in the lives of those suffering from hunger. Helping to feed the hungry not only has a direct impact on their lives, but it can also lead to social and economic development in communities by reducing poverty and improving health outcomes. Doing something for the world by supporting Feed the Hungry is, therefore, a worthwhile and impactful endeavor.

105. Help a stranger

We can help a stranger in many ways, such as offering to carry their grocery bags, helping them change a tire, or simply offering a listening ear. Engaging in small acts of kindness can have a powerful impact on someone's day and may even brighten their outlook on life. Additionally, donating to charities that support those in need can make a significant difference in the lives of strangers. The simple act of helping another person can be incredibly rewarding and is a testament to our shared humanity.

One simple way to help is to offer assistance with carrying or lifting heavy items. If someone seems lost or confused, provide directions or offer to escort them to their destination. You can also offer a listening ear or a smile to brighten their day. Donate to charities or volunteer in your community to help those in need. Remember to always be aware of your surroundings and trust your gut instincts when lending a hand.

106. Volunteer for a cause you believe in.

Volunteering for a cause you believe in can help you open your heart and give back to the community. When you dedicate your time and energy to a cause, you create a sense of purpose and fulfillment in your life. It allows you to connect with other like-minded individuals who share your values and beliefs, making you feel more connected to the world around you. By volunteering, you can make a difference in the lives of others, while also improving your own mental and emotional well-being. So, find a cause that you're passionate about and start volunteering today!

107. Help other people shine

The truest measure of success is not in our own accomplishments, but in how we help others achieve theirs. One way to do this is to be a supportive and encouraging presence in their lives, offering constructive feedback and uplifting words whenever possible. Additionally, we can help connect people with resources, opportunities, and networks that will help them achieve their goals.

By helping others shine, we can create a more equal, collaborative, and vibrant community where everyone has the chance to thrive.

How to help other People shine?

1. Give them opportunities to showcase their skills and talents.

2. Encourage them to speak up and share their ideas in team meetings.

3. Acknowledge and appreciate their efforts and achievements.

4. Offer constructive feedback and help them improve their performance.

5. Collaborate with them on projects and highlight their contributions.

6. Share their accomplishments and successes with others in the organization.

108. Have an open ear

It's crucial to have an open ear to support those who need it. Listening without judgment, offering empathy, and showing encouragement can make a world of difference to someone who may be struggling. Creating a safe space where individuals feel comfortable to share their thoughts, feelings, and concerns can help alleviate stress and anxiety. It's important to recognize the power of being present and actively engaged in conversations that can help someone in need. By offering support and understanding, we can create a positive impact on someone's well-being and mental health.

109. Spend time with children.

Spending time with children has numerous benefits, including the ability to open the heart.

Children have a way of bringing out the best in people, reminding us of our capacity for joy, wonder, and playfulness. They can melt away stress and worry, offer unconditional love and acceptance, and boost self-esteem. They can also inspire us to be more creative, patient, and kind, fostering a greater sense of empathy and compassion. Ultimately, the time we spend with children can be both healing and transformational, helping us to reconnect with our deepest selves and our shared humanity.

Examples to spend time with children.

Reading:

Engaging in a reading session with children can both strengthen literacy skills and create an opportunity for bonding.

"The True Story of the Three Little Pigs"
"Charlie and the Chocolate Factory" by Roald Dahl
"Harry Potter and the Philosopher's Stone" by J.K. Rowling

2. Arts and crafts:

Encouraging children to explore their creativity through art can promote self-expression and showcase their unique perspectives.

3. Outdoor activities:

Spending time outside, whether it be playing games, going for a nature walk, or simply enjoying the fresh air, can promote physical activity and reduce stress.

Nature walks: explore a local park or nature reserve.

Gardening: plant and maintain a small garden of flowers, vegetables, or herbs.

Sports: play soccer, basketball, or other team sports.

Water play: go swimming, rafting, or kayaking.

4. Cooking:

Cooking with children can teach important life skills while also fostering a sense of teamwork and accomplishment.

One quick and easy recipe for kids is a homemade pizza bagel.

Here are the steps:

1. Preheat the oven to 375°F.

2. Slice a bagel in half and place it on a baking sheet.

3. Spread tomato sauce on each half of the bagel.

4. Sprinkle shredded cheese over the sauce.

5. Add any desired toppings such as sliced pepperoni or sausage, diced onions, bell peppers, or mushrooms.

6. Bake in the preheated oven for 10-12 minutes until the cheese is melted and bubbly.

7. Let cool for a few minutes before serving.

This recipe is a delicious and fun way to get kids involved in the kitchen and encourages creativity in choosing toppings.

5. Playing games:

Whether it be board games, card games, or outdoor games, playing together can help develop social skills and create lasting memories

1. Mensch ärgere Dich nicht
2. Räuber Hotzenplotz
3. Blinde Kuh:

110.   Don't charge

We welcome and embrace everyone, regardless of their background or circumstances. Our policy is to provide equal opportunities to all, without any form of discrimination or prejudice. Our goal is to create an inclusive and compassionate environment where all individuals feel valued and respected. We believe in the power of diversity and strive to promote unity and harmony among all members of society.

111. Reduce your carbon footprint

Reducing your carbon footprint can be done in several ways. One of the most effective strategies is to reduce energy use. This can be achieved by turning off lights and appliances when not in use, using public transport or carpooling, and purchasing energy-efficient products. Additionally, reducing water consumption, recycling, and eating less meat can also decrease your carbon footprint. Planting trees can also help to offset the carbon emissions that contribute to climate change. Being mindful of your daily choices and making small changes can make a significant impact on reducing your carbon footprint.

Afterword

I hope that the 111 steps you have taken with me will bring you closer to the opening of your heart. Remember that the journey towards self-love and inner peace is ongoing, and that each step you take is progress. Always be gentle with yourself, take breaks when necessary, and continue to do the inner work.

Carry the lessons and practices with you in every aspect of your life, and continue to show compassion and kindness to yourself and others. Embrace vulnerability and allow yourself to truly feel and connect with the world around you. May this book serve as a guide on your path to a more open heart, and may you continue to grow and flourish in love.

Thank you for allowing me to be a part of your journey, and I wish you all the best on your path towards an open heart.

Love, Diana

Sources and Links

1. Beliefnet.com - https://www.beliefnet.com/health/healing-heart.aspx
2. Hayhouse.com - https://www.hayhouse.com/healing-heart/
3. Chopra.com - https://chopra.com/articles/heart-healing-the-four-keys-to-an-awakened-heart
4. Theheartysoul.com - https://theheartysoul.com/
5. Gaiam.com - https://www.gaiam.com/blogs/discover/7-ways-to-heal-your-spiritual-heart
6. Mindbodygreen.com - https://www.mindbodygreen.com/0-27673/how-to-heal-a-broken-heart-spiritually.html
7. Spiritualityandpractice.com - https://www.spiritualityandpractice.com/practices/features/view/28482/the-spiritual-practice-of-a-healthy-heart
8. Wanderlust.com - https://wanderlust.com/journal/6-ways-to-heal-your-heart-chakra/
9. Gaia.com - https://www.gaia.com/article/5-ways-to-heal-your-heart-chakra
10. Elephanjournal.com - https://www.elephantjournal.com/2019/07/the-spiritual-wounds-of-the-heart-how-to-recover-from-the-pain/
11.Heartmath.com

About the Author
Diana Krauss

"111 Steps to Open the Heart", written by renowned, masterchef chef, healer and spiritual teacher, Diana Krauss, presents a step-by-step guide to unleashing the power of the heart, cultivating inner peace, and living life to the fullest.

After two major transformative experience, something shifted within me and my heart opened wide.

This experience allowed me to see the world in a completely new way and altered my perspective on life.

I found myself feeling more loving, connected and vulnerable than ever before.

This transition led me down a path of self-discovery and personal growth, helping me realise the power of love and the beauty of opening up to others.